Sage:

A Lark's Story

ISBN: 1491028718

ISBN 13: 9781491028711

Library of Congress Control Number: 2013913506

CreateSpace Independent Publishing Platform, North Charleston, SC

Sage:

A Lark's Story

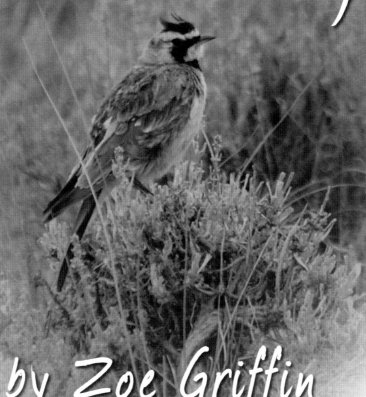

by Zoe Griffin

This Book is dedicated to Betty Boehm, who introduced me to the horned lark, and is one of my great birding friends. Thank you for bringing me into birding and the horned lark world.

I would like to give a special thank you to Heather Preble, who really encouraged me to write and helped me along with this book. Thank you, I couldn't have done this without you.

TABLE OF CONTENTS

Hello

Hello. My name is Sage, the horned lark. I am an amazing little bird and I am going to tell you my life story in this book. Now follow me as you enter my world, the world of a bird, the world of a horned lark.

CHAPTER ONE

My Appearance

I am a small, sparrow-like bird that is known as a songbird. I am also known as a passerine. That means a four-toed perching bird. I have a black chest patch to go along with my black face patch. My back, the crown of my head, and the back of my neck are pale brown. My throat, the most colorful part of me, is a beautiful yellow color, but some of my friends' throat plumage is paler. Our coloration varies depending on our gender and our habitat. Males, like my mate and his buddies, tend to be more colorful so they can show off for us females. To go with my magnificent blend of body colors, I have two feather "horns" that stick out of the crown of my head. The males use those horns to attract a mate and to scare off other birds and predators. Now you know how I got my name and what I look like!

If you want to know about my babies' feather patterns, well, you are in luck! My babies (known as chicks) look quite similar to me, but there are some major differences. My babies will have the same face pattern that I have, but the pattern will be fainter than mine. My chicks will not have the feather horns as I do; those will form as they get older. The chicks have black streaks on their chests, and they have pale white spots on the crowns of their heads, on their backs, and on the backs of their necks where my magnificent feathers are light brown.

My Other Names

In some states and to some people, my species is called something else. A hunter calls me a bean bird, probably because I'm pretty small, like a bean compared to other birds. People in California call me a reed bird. I am sometimes called a shore lark. Scientists or those who use my scientific name call me *Eremophila alpestris*.

Wow! Amazing, isn't it? I am known by so many names besides horned lark! Now that you know the details of my appearance and other names that I am known by, let us move on to my parenting life—the part about my chicks, my prized jewels.

Look at my beautiful colors! Do you see my fluffy little horns?

Chapter Two

Family and Parenting Life

We horned larks, like all good parents, care for our young to the best of our ability. August to November is our breeding season. When I went to the breeding grounds, I met my special mate, Joe. He did a courtship dance for me. First, he flew in the air and got up to about eight hundred feet. Then, he circled above me and sang me a song. After that, he dove down toward the ground, wings tucked to his sides. At the last second before crashing, he opened his wings and pulled up, and then landed beside me. He then strutted around me with his horns stuck in the air. I couldn't resist. We became mates for life. We then headed to breed in grasslands and nest on the ground. Before laying my eggs, I let Joe choose an area that he can protect while I raise our chicks. Then, Joe, will let me choose part of his protected area for my nest.

I make a cup out of grass to use as my nest. Before I lay my eggs, I eat quite a lot of grain and insects (see chapter three)—I have a feast of sorts—so that my babies will be strong and healthy when they hatch. Then, I lay three or four speckled eggs that can be anywhere from grey to green. My eggs are less than an inch long. They measure 0.8 inch, to be exact. I incubate my eggs for eleven to sixteen days, and after that, my eggs will hatch! My new babies will emerge from the eggs in the nest.

This season, I laid four eggs, and I named my children Payton, Mindy, Robert, and Carly. After they hatched, I fed them a nice meal of bugs and grains and then fluffed up my feathers around them to keep them warm while they napped, safe and sound.

Sometimes, a cowbird will lay her eggs in my girlfriends' nests. After laying, the cowbird will leave, letting the already busy horned lark mothers take care of the cowbird chicks as well as their own! The baby larks get very little food and starve while the cowbirds thrive because they are larger. The poor, poor baby larks!

As my young grow up, they will get better nourishment on their own and I will take care of them less and less. After they learn how to hunt and foriage, I will let them out of the nest to live on their own, but Joe and I still help to feed them for a while. My chicks will not be chicks any more. They will be juveniles (jü-və-ˌnī(-ə)l). This means that they are not adults, but they are old enough to care for themselves. After that, we will join flocks (or groups) of our own species. (See Chapter 3 for more about flocks.)

Joe keeping his eyes out for predators.
He's so loyal and keeps the family safe all day.

CHAPTER THREE

Habitat and Lifestyle

We horned larks like to stick together. We will form groups called flocks. We will flock in the type of environment we like, which is grassy plains or sage fields (which my mother named me after- I was raised and raised my kids in one of these sage fields). When we flock, we sometimes decide to join flocks of other species. These species include the snow bunting, the dark-eyed junco, the Lapland longspurs, and the American pipit.

Food Habits

We horned larks eat a variety of weeds, including grain, weed seeds, green and yellow foxtail, bur clover, Napa thistle, corn cockle, and buttonweed. We are very helpful to farmers because instead of simply pecking apart the heads of the harmful weeds like other bird species do, we eat the entire head. This is helpful to farmers because it prevents the seeds from the weeds from spreading and ruining the farmer's crops. Out of the one hundred most harmful weeds in the United States, we eat thirty-eight of those varieties! We are cute and helpful too!

We also eat insects. The insects we eat include beetles, butterflies, grasshoppers, moths, ants, spiders, flies, and termites. We eat very few insects in the winter because insects die off in the cold. The insect that we eat most often is the weevil. We not only eat the adult bugs, but we also eat the eggs, larvae, and the cocoons. Weevils have a good camouflage trick—they roll over onto their backs and play dead, blending in with the ground. But their camo is not good enough! We have sharp, little eyes and can see the weevils! We can catch them and gobble up a little weevil snack!

I'm preparing for lunch. Just a searchin' for the weevils.

CHAPTER FOUR

Survival

In order to survive, there are some things that we have to do. For example, our coloring and our horns provide camouflage and protection from predators. Some of the predators that eat us include the red-tailed hawk, the red-shouldered hawk, the marsh hawk, the prairie falcon, the burrowing owl, the screech owl, skunks, raccoons, and domestic cats.

Sometimes we bury ourselves in the snow when the temperature is extremely cold so that we can maintain our body temperature, just like our ruffed grouse friends do. I wonder if we copied the ruffed grouse, or if the ruffed grouse copied us? Ha ha! Just kidding.

At one time, people hunted us for food. But eventually people saw our value and stopped hunting us. The reason is that we eat insects and weeds that are harmful to people's crops. Hooray for the food that we eat! Those foods saved our lives!

In some states, we are protected by the United States government because we are running out of room to nest because of new buildings being put in.

See how I blend in with my surroundings? That's one way I survive.

CHAPTER FIVE

Activities at Home

If you want to learn more about us horned larks, try the activities in this chapter!

ACTIVITY #1

The Weight Test

Materials:

- A gram scale
- Twenty-six small paper clips

1. Hold the paper clips in your hand. See how heavy they feel.

2. Put the paper clips on the scale. See how many grams they weigh.

3. You have held the weight of a horned lark like me in your hand!

Yes, that's right. We horned larks weigh as much as twenty-six small paper clips do!

ACTIVITY #2

Make a Horned Lark Egg

Materials:

- A paper cup
- 2 tablespoons flour
- 1 tablespoon water
- Ruler
- A black marker

1. Mix the flour and the water in the cup. If your mixture is too wet, add a bit more flour. If it's too dry, add a bit more water.

2. Take out a small ball of the goo and form it into an egg shape. Make sure that the egg is not really skinny. Make it like an egg but it still has to be small!

3. Using your ruler, make sure that the "egg" is 0.8 inches long (2.032 centimeters).

4. Let the egg dry for at least 1½ days. When it is dry, use your marker to draw some black speckles on the egg.

My egg is tiny! Don't you agree? You are holding a model of my egg in your hand! Cool, huh?

ACTIVITY #3

Camoflauge Test

Materials:

- Your eyes
- Your keen senses

Take a close look at this picture of me. Try and find me. If you can't find me, that means my feathers are working to protect me and camoflauge me! I am there, I promise! Ask your parents or siblings if you need help.

Do you see me now? If you had found me on the previous page, great job! I hope you had a great time reading about me and trying out my fun activities. See you soon!

Good-Bye!

I would like to thank you for reading about me and my life as a bird. My mate, Joe, and I are happy and so are our four chicks, Payton, Mindy, Robert, and Carly. Our children have chicks of their own! Now, I have to go and get myself some yummy dinner of weevils and noxious weeds! Good-bye from me and my family, and we hope to see you again soon.

References

1. Waldo Lee Mcatee, *Horned Larks and Their Relation to Agriculture* (Lavergne, TN:Nabu Public Domain Reprints, 1913) 35 pages

2. Douglas W. Faulkner, *Birds of Wyoming* (Greenwood Village, CO:Roberts and Company Publishers,2010) 403 pages

3. Edward S. Brinkley, *Field Guide to Bird of North America* (New York, NY:Sterling Publishing Co. Inc., 2007) 527 pages

4. Christopher M. Perrins and Alex L. A. Middleton, *The Encyclopedia of Birds* (Oxford,New York:The Brown Reference Group, 2003) 655 pages

5. Boehm, Elizabeth. Telephone Interview. 3/20/13.

6. Lillrose, Michael. Telephone Interview. 3/19/13.

7. Patla, Susan. Telephone Interview. 4/4/13

8. "Horned Lark", Last Modified June 4,2013 http://en.wikipedia.org/wiki/Eremophila_alpestris#Description

9. "Horned Lark" http://www.allaboutbirds.org/guide/Horned_Lark/id

10. "Horned Lark Eremophila Alpestris" http://www.mbr-pwrc.usgs.gov/id/framlst/i4740id.html

11. "Horned Lark" http://www.birdinginformation.com/birds/larks/horned-lark/

12. "Horned Lark" http://www.birdweb.org/birdweb/bird/horned_lark

13. "Horned Lark"http://www.biokids.umich.edu/critters/Eremophila_alpestris/

14. "Horned Lark"http://www.birdzilla.com/birds/Horned-Lark/home.html

15. "Horned Lark Eremophila Alpestris"http://www.audubonbirds.org/species/Birds/Horned-Lark.html

16. Horned Lark http://www.birdingbirds.com/encyclopedia/horned-lark.htm

Made in the USA
Charleston, SC
12 October 2013